WISDOM

summersdale

WISDOM

Summersdale Publishers Ltd
46 West Street
Chichester
West Sussex
PO19 1RP
UK

www.summersdale.com

Printed and bound in China

ISBN: 978-1-84953-383-6

Substantial discounts on bulk quantities of Summersdale books are available to corporations, professional associations and other organisations. For details contact Nicky Douglas by telephone: +44 (0) 1243 756902, fax: +44 (0) 1243 786300 or email: nicky@summersdale.com.

To...

From...

Introduction

Wisdom does not come from a single source, but rather from your experience with the people and world around you. This book is filled with quotations to inspire and enlighten you, along with mindful tips to help light a path to finding wisdom, wherever you are, at any time of day. Enjoy discovering the pleasures of an open and thoughtful approach to life.

Make each day both
useful and pleasant,
and prove that you
understand the worth
of time by employing
it well.

Louisa May Alcott

Listen to your inner wisdom as you know yourself best of all.

You must be the change you want to see in the world.

Mahatma Gandhi

IT TAKES COURAGE
TO FACE ONE'S
OWN SHORTCOMINGS,
AND WISDOM TO
DO SOMETHING
ABOUT THEM.

Edgar Cayce

We are made wise not by the recollection of our past, but by the responsibility for our future.

George Bernard Shaw

The highest
form of wisdom is
kindness.

The Talmud

There are three
ingredients in the
good life: learning,
earning and yearning.

Christopher Morley

Knowledge comes but
wisdom lingers.

Alfred, Lord Tennyson

*Keep a journal
in which you can
write about your
choices, decisions and
experiences.*

WE CARRY
WITHIN US THE
WONDERS
WE SEEK
WITHOUT US.

Sir Thomas Browne

The greater the
obstacle, the
more glory in
overcoming it.

Molière

Our lives begin to end the day we become silent about things that matter.

Martin Luther King Jr

Wise men learn
many things from
their enemies.

Aristophanes

The more we see,
the more we are
capable of seeing.

Maria Mitchell

True religion is real living; living with all one's soul, with all one's goodness and righteousness.

Albert Einstein

The most decisive
actions of our life...
are most often
unconsidered actions.

André Gide

BE HAPPY.
IT'S ONE WAY OF
BEING WISE.

Colette

Notice things you are grateful for every day.

Science is organised
knowledge.
Wisdom is organised
life.

Immanuel Kant

If your compassion
does not include
yourself, it is
incomplete.

Siddhārtha Gautama Buddha

You cannot find peace
by avoiding life.

Virginia Woolf

It is not because things
are difficult that we
do not dare; it
is because we do not
dare that they are
difficult.

Seneca

We learn wisdom
from failure much
more than success.

Samuel Smiles

By attempting the impossible one can attain the highest level of the possible.

August Strindberg

THE HIGHEST RESULT OF EDUCATION IS TOLERANCE.

Helen Keller

*When you meet
anyone at all, notice
their good qualities
and look for things
you have in common.
There will always
be some!*

The good life is one inspired by love and guided by knowledge.

Bertrand Russell

Kindness is
more important than
wisdom, and the
recognition of this
is the beginning of
wisdom.

Theodore Rubin

Only a life lived
for others is a life
worthwhile.

Albert Einstein

We make a living
by what we get, but
we make a life by
what we give.

Winston Churchill

It is strange how
often a heart must
be broken before the
years can make
it wise.

Sara Teasdale

Knowledge is a
process of piling up
facts; wisdom lies in
their simplification.

Martin Fischer

It's more important to
do the right thing than
to do things right.

Peter Drucker

*Trust your intuition
and be brave enough
not to follow
the crowd.*

WONDER IS THE BEGINNING OF WISDOM.

Socrates

Dare to be wise: when
you begin you are
already halfway there.

Horace

Beauty endures
only for as long as it
can be seen; goodness,
beautiful today,
will remain so
tomorrow.

Sappho

Speak few words,
but say them with
quietude and sincerity
and they will be
long-lasting.

Lao Tzu

Vanity is the
quicksand of reason.

George Sand

All human wisdom
is summed up in two
words – wait and
hope.

Alexandre Dumas *père*

You're already a wise person if you know that being kind is always the right choice.

Nothing happens
unless first we dream.

Carl Sandburg

LIFE IS LIKE PLAYING A VIOLIN SOLO IN PUBLIC, AND LEARNING THE INSTRUMENT AS ONE GOES ON.

Samuel Butler

Patience is
the companion
of wisdom.

St Augustine of Hippo

If you do not tell the
truth about yourself
you cannot tell it
about other people.

Virginia Woolf

What is the meaning
of life? To be happy
and useful.

Dalai Lama

It is cowardice to
perceive what is right
but not to do it.

Confucius

Courage without conscience is a wild beast.

Robert G. Ingersoll

People grow through experience if they meet life honestly and courageously. This is how character is built.

Eleanor Roosevelt

*Let your friends
know that they can
depend on your
support and presence.*

No act of kindness, no
matter how small, is
ever wasted.

Aesop

REJECT YOUR SENSE OF INJURY AND THE INJURY ITSELF DISAPPEARS.

Marcus Aurelius

One must be poor
to know the luxury
of giving.

George Eliot

When you are good
to others you are best
to yourself.

Benjamin Franklin

He who masters
others has power. He
who masters himself
has strength.

Lao Tzu

Life begets life. Energy
creates energy. It is by
spending oneself that
one becomes rich.

Sarah Bernhardt

As soon as you trust yourself, you will know how to live.

Johann Wolfgang von Goethe

*Patience! All
things happen at the
perfect time.*

You cannot run away from weakness; you must some time fight it out or perish.

Robert Louis Stevenson

IF YOU HAVE KNOWLEDGE, LET OTHERS LIGHT THEIR CANDLES IN IT.

Margaret Fuller

Power without
wisdom collapses
under its own weight.

Horace

The greatest mistake you can make in life is to be continually fearing you will make one.

Elbert Hubbard

Never apologise
for showing feeling.
When you do so,
you apologise for
the truth.

Benjamin Disraeli

The truest greatness
lies in being kind, the
truest wisdom in a
happy mind.

Ella Wheeler Wilcox

A wise man turns chance into good fortune.

Thomas Fuller

Allow others to express their opinions. You don't have to agree and you have the right to remain silent.

Memory is the mother
of all wisdom.

Aeschylus

The only certainty is that nothing is certain.

Pliny the Elder

HE WHO KNOWS OTHERS IS LEARNED; HE WHO KNOWS HIMSELF IS WISE.

Lao Tzu

Life was meant to be lived and curiosity must be kept alive. One must never, for whatever reason, turn his back on life.

Eleanor Roosevelt

The real voyage of discovery consists not in seeking new landscapes but in having new eyes.

Marcel Proust

Wisdom is oftentimes nearer when we stoop than when we soar.

William Wordsworth

There is not a heart but has its moments of longing, yearning for something better, nobler, holier than it knows now.

Henry Ward Beecher

The surest test
of discipline is
its absence.

Clara Barton

Let go of old experiences and unhealthy past relationships. Allow yourself to move on to new things.

Honesty is the first chapter in the book of wisdom.

Thomas Jefferson

THERE IS NOTHING THAT WILL NOT REVEAL ITS SECRETS IF YOU LOVE IT ENOUGH.

George Washington Carver

The strongest
principle of growth
lies in human choice.

George Eliot

To conquer
fear is the beginning
of wisdom.

Bertrand Russell

The only gift is a
portion of thyself.

Ralph Waldo Emerson

A wise man makes his own decisions; an ignorant man follows the public opinion.

Chinese proverb

All men by
nature desire
knowledge.

Aristotle

When a person criticises you unkindly, remember, it will reflect something from within them and may not even be about you at all.

DO WHAT YOU CAN, WITH WHAT YOU HAVE, WHERE YOU ARE.

Theodore Roosevelt

Wise men talk
because they have
something to say;
fools, because they
have to say something.

Plato

Without courage,
wisdom bears no fruit.

Baltasar Gracián

Listen or your tongue
will keep you deaf.

Native American proverb

I think one's feelings
waste themselves in
words; they ought
all to be distilled into
actions and into
actions which bring
results.

Florence Nightingale

Some of the wisest words you will ever hear will come from children. Take time to listen and think about what they say.

BE NOT AFRAID OF LIFE. BELIEVE THAT LIFE IS WORTH LIVING, AND YOUR BELIEF WILL HELP CREATE THE FACT.

Henry James

If you're interested in finding out more
about our gift books, follow us on Twitter:
@Summersdale

www.summersdale.com